Technology of Skilled Processes

Basic Engineering Competences

Joining

Editorial Panel

J Braddock, CEng, MWeld I, MISMW, Cert Ed

D J Butterworth, BSc, MSc, TEng, MIAgE

N A Butterworth, MSc, CGIA, CEng, FIMechE, FIProdE

V Green, TEng(CEI), MBIM
Head of Department of Engineering Crafts,
Huddersfield Technical College

D Streets, MSc, CEng, MIProdE

C Sutcliffe, OBE, MSc, CEng, MIMechE
Vocational Curriculum Services
City and Guilds of London Institute

Published as a
co-operative venture
between
Stam Press Ltd

and
City and Guilds

Technology of Skilled Processes 367-1

Section	Process	Section	Process
1	Observing Safe Practices	8	Joining
2	Moving Loads	9	Fabrication
3	Measurement and Dimensional Control (1)	10	Soft Soldering, Hard Soldering and Brazing
4	Marking Out	11	Fusion Welding
5	Work and Toolholding	12	Power Transmission
6	Removing Material	13	Assembly and Dismantling (1)
7	Forming	14	Interpreting Drawings, Specifications and Data

Basic Engineering Competences 201

Basic Engineering Technology
201-1-01
01 Industrial Studies
02 Observing Safe Practices
03 Moving Loads
04 Measurement and Dimensional Control (1)
05 Marking Out
06 Work and Toolholding
07 Removing Material
08 Joining
09 Interpreting Drawings, Specifications and Data
010 Assembly and Dismantling (1)

Basic Fabrication and Welding Technology
201-1-07
01 Forming
02 Fabrication
03 Soft Soldering, Hard Soldering and Brazing
04 Fusion Welding

Basic Maintenance Technology
201-1-09
01 Forming
02 Soft Soldering, Hard Soldering and Brazing
03 Power Transmission
04 Measurement and Testing of Electro-Mechanical Systems (1)

Science Background to Technology
201-1-04
01 Basic Physical Quantities, Electricity and Magnetism
02 Forces
03 Pressure
04 The Principles of Tool Construction; Materials Technology

SUPPORTING BOOKS

Book titles	Covering	Covering
Basic Engineering	**Syllabus** 367-1	Syllabus 201-1-01
Observing Safe Practices and Moving Loads	Section 1 and 2	02-03
Measuring and Marking Out	Section 3 and 4	04-05
Workholding and Toolholding: Removing Material	Section 5 and 6	06-07
Joining	Section 8	08
Interpreting Drawings, Specifications and Data	Section 14	09
Assembling and Dismantling	Section 13	10
Fabrication and Welding		Syllabus 201-1-07
Forming	Section 7	01
Fabrication	Section 9	02
Soft Soldering, Hard Soldering and Brazing	Section 10	03
Fusion Welding	Section 11	04
Maintenance		Syllabus 201-1-09
Forming	Section 7	01
Soft Soldering, Hard Soldering and Brazing	Section 10	02
Power Transmission	Section 12	03
Science		Syllabus 201-1-04
Basic Physical Quantities, Electricity and Magnetism		01
Forces		02
Pressure		03
Principles of Tool Construction; Material Technology		04

201 – Basic Engineering Competences
201-1-01 Basic Engineering Technology

08 Basic Competence in Joining

The contents of this book have been designed to cover the requirements of the City and Guilds Basic Process Competence Syllabus (367-1), section 8. The contents of the component 08 of the City and Guilds Basic Engineering Technology Syllabus 201-1-01 are identical and thus equally covered by this book.

As listed, the heading references in this book conform with those in the syllabus section 8 scheme 367-1. In the 201 scheme syllabus items are numbered sequentially and prefixed with the component number, e.g. item 1 in syllabus 08 is 8.1.

Below, in brackets following the page numbers, we give the 201 syllabus sequence numbers.

Contents

4 Introduction

This book is intended for those who are, or will be, doing a practical job in industry.

It is specially written for those who need technology as a background to their work and as a means of adapting to changes in working practices caused by technological advance. Where words such as 'he' or ''craftsman' appear in this series, they are to be inter-preted as 'he/she', 'craftsman/woman'.

This new series of textbooks presents the technology in terms of competence rather than working from a conventional theoretical base, i.e. the material will help readers understand:

- the use of
- the change to
- the development of
- other uses of

industrial process technology and skills.

This book has been compiled after a survey of the industrial skilled processes which form the nucleus of occupational schemes and pre-vocational courses of the City and Guilds of London Institute and a comparison with provisions elsewhere in Europe.

Three basic facts emerged:

- the technology is common to many different schemes though the contexts of applications are very different;

- the technology is being taught in a variety of work-shops in a variety of exercises related to the immediate needs of students and their industries; these industrially-related exercises formed excellent learning tasks and provided clear motivation for students because of their immediate relevance;
- the technology is so well integrated with the 'first-task need' that students did not recognise its relevance to many other tasks they would be called upon to perform.

This book seeks to build on the learning tasks and to provide a means of learning and generalising technology, so that the immediate job is better under-stood and better done, new tasks using the same process technology are more quickly mastered and updating or retraining is easier and more effective.

The editors would welcome further constructive suggestions which should be addressed to:
Stam Press Ltd
Old Station Drive
Leckhampton
Cheltenham
GL53 0DN

ACKNOWLEDGEMENTS

The publishers gladly record their thanks to the following contributors who have kindly supplied material for inclusion in this book:

Fabrication and Welding by W. Kenyon; Longman Group Ltd.; The Engineering Industry Training Board

ISBN 0 85973 021 2

Printed and bound in Great Britain
by Martin's of Berwick.

First published in Great Britain 1987
as a co-operative venture between Stam Press Ltd
and the City and Guilds of London Institute

Reprinted 1988

Project Structure and Use of Syllabus Bank and Supporting Books

1   The TECHNOLOGY associated with a given industrial process is a common requirement, but the APPLICATIONS vary by occupation and task, so a distinction has to be made between:

(a)   THE AIM of the process: eg. to bend, metals, to drill, etc.

(b)   THE LEARNING and ASSESSMENT: related to the application(s) specific to the industry to which the candidate belongs or aspires, or to the context of scheme chosen as a basis of study.

2   The approach suggested for the learning and assessment of any process technology is as follows:

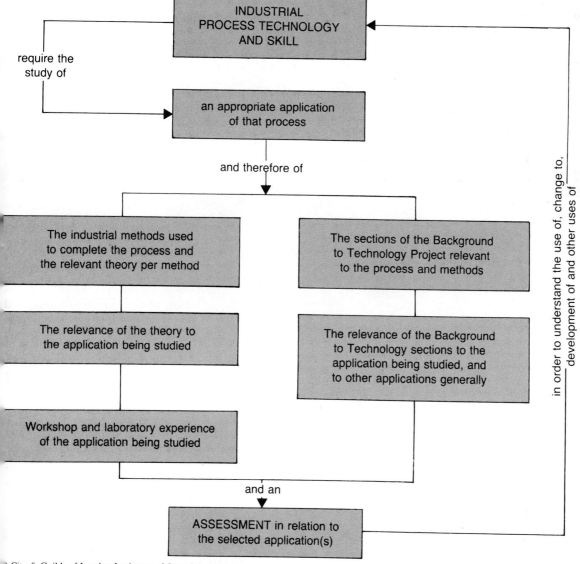

) City & Guilds of London Institute and Stam Press Ltd

1 Joining

1.a Purpose of joining

The purpose of joining, in the technological sense, is to secure individual components in order to produce a desired fabrication. Joints are classified in one or other of the following categories:

- *permanent* (e.g. hard soldered, welded, riveted, joined by adhesives, Fig. **1.**1)
- *temporary* (e.g. soft soldered, screwed/bolted, pinned, Fig. **1.**2)

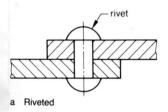

a   Riveted

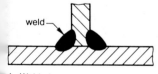

b   Brazed (hard soldered)

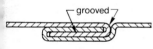

c   Grooved

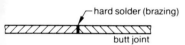

d   Welded

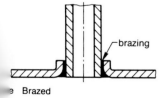

e   Brazed

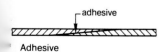

Adhesive

1.1   Typical permanent joints

a   Soft soldered

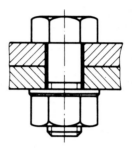

b   Bolted

c   Pinned

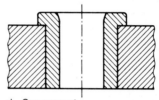

d   Compressed

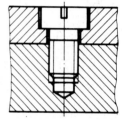

e   Screwed

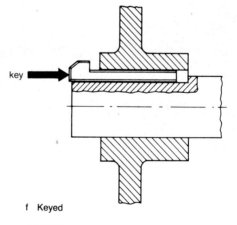

f   Keyed

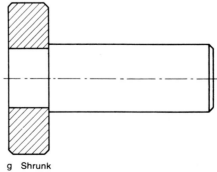

g   Shrunk

1.2   Typical temporary joints

• *flexible* (e.g. couplings, hinges, Fig. **1.**3)

This book does not set out to provide the student with detailed instructions on the procedures to be followed when making any of the joints described. It provides an overview of the various joints used in industry and explains why one joint is more suited to a particular purpose than is another. More detailed descriptions of the joining process can be found in the following books in the 'Technology of Skilled Processes' series:

• *Fabrication* (Section 9)
• *Soft Soldering, Hard Soldering, and Brazing* (Section 10)
• *Fusion Welding* (Section 11)

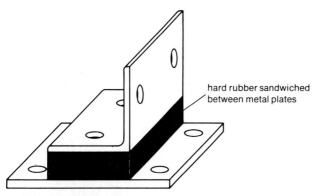

a   A simple engine mounting

hard rubber sandwiched between metal plates

d   Universal joint

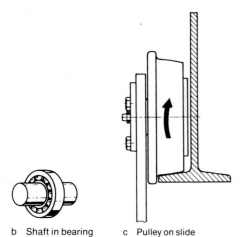

b   Shaft in bearing   c   Pulley on slide

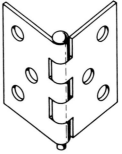

e   Hinge

1.3   Typical flexible joints

2 Range of joints

2.a Permanent joints

A joint is permanent if one or more of the components, or the medium joining them, has to be damaged in order to separate them, e.g.:
- riveted
- welded
- soldered/brazed (note, however, that soft soldered joints can be temporary)
- joined by adhesives.

2.b Temporary joints

A joint is temporary if one or more of the components can be separated without damage and re-assembled, generally using the same fastener, e.g.:
- screwed or bolted
- pinned or keyed

- shrunk
- compressed.

Note, however, that engineering tolerances are such that some shrunk and compressed joints may not be separated without damage and are then classified as permanent joints.

2.c Flexible joints

A joint is flexible if it permits the components that are joined to move relative to each other, e.g.:
- coupling
- hinge
- shafts in bearings
- slides (on or in guides).

Flexible joints may be either permanent or temporary. Some types of flexible joints are shown in Fig. 1.3.

3 Methods of joining

3.a Soldering

Soldering is defined as: the hot joining of metals by adhesion using, as a thin film between the parts to be joined, a metallic bonding alloy having a relatively low melting point.

Note: Soldering does not involve any fusion in the materials being joined.

There are two types of soldering process: soft soldering and brazing (variously called hard soldering or silver soldering). The choice between the two methods depends on the requirements of the joint. As a general rule it can be stated that a soft solder may be used where mechanical strength is not the first consideration, e.g. electrical connections, tin plate fabrication or pipe connections. A brazed joint will be used where mechanical strength is of prime importance, e.g. lightweight fabrications in non-ferrous metals. The following metals are suitable for joining by soldering: copper, nickel, tin, iron, lead, zinc, aluminium and many of their alloys. Aluminium, however, is difficult to solder, the technique required is precise and working with aluminium is best left to a person with considerable experience of soldering.

The basic difference in the techniques for soft soldering and brazing is:

- **Soft soldering** – heat is usually applied to the joint by means of a heated 'soldering bit', normally of shaped copper.
- **Brazing** – heat is applied directly to the joint by a naked flame carbon arc. A hard solder will not melt below red heat.

Note: In industry other forms of heating are available. The series book *Soft Soldering, Hard Soldering and Brazing* should be studied for information on industrial heating.

3.a. i. Soft soldering

Soft solders are alloys of tin and lead with other elements, such as antimony and bismuth, added to give further properties to the solder. The melting point is relatively low (between 183°C and 255°C). In general, the higher the proportion of lead in the solder the wider the solidification range. BS 219 lists and grades the range of soft solders and gives examples of their use.

Note: The solidification range of a solder is the temperature range between that at which a solder melts and that at which it solidifies.

Table 3.1 lists three of the most common grades and gives their typical use.

3.a. i. 1 Materials required

The following tools and materials should be available before any soldering is attempted:

- soldering iron (Fig. 3.1)
- source of heat – gas flame, blow lamp (unless an electric soldering iron is being used)
- flux – type dependent on joining to be done. Zinc chloride, a liquid flux is suitable for most metals. Where it is important to avoid corrosion e.g. applications involving an electric current path, a proprietary non-corrosive resin or resin cored solder must be used.
- solder – grade dependent on joining to be done (see Table 3.1 or BS 219)
- cleaning equipment, e.g. file, rag, etc.

Table 3.1 Typical soft solders

Grade	Maximum tin content	Remainder lead content	Maximum antimony	Solidification temperature	Liquid temperature	Use
K	60%	39.5%	0.5%	183°C	188°C	Fine electrical and tinsmith
F	50%	49.5%	0.5%	183°C	212°C	General
J	30%	69.7%	0.3%	183°C	255°C	Plumbing (wiped joints)

3.a. i. 2 Procedure

The procedure to be followed is fully described in the series book *Soft Soldering, Hard Soldering and Brazing* (Section 10).
The following points are essential to that procedure:

- the soldering iron must be cleaned and tinned, i.e., have a film of solder on its surface
- the surfaces to be joined must be thoroughly cleaned, i.e. any grease, rust or corrosion must be removed
- any infusible oxide film on the surfaces to be joined must be dissolved by the application of a suitable flux (the film would prevent adhesion)
- the surfaces to be joined must be lapped, i.e. the parts to be joined must lie over each other.

3.a. i. 3 Faults

The most common fault that arises during a soldering operation is a 'dry joint'. This occurs when the surfaces are not prepared correctly, insufficient heat is applied to the joint or the materials being joined are moved before the solder has solidified.

3.a. ii Brazing

The term brazing is generally used to cover a range of joining processes in which the parent metal is not deliberately melted, but the temperature needed greatly exceeds that required for soft soldering. This process may also be called hard or silver soldering.
The process of hard soldering is very similar to that of soft soldering in that the area of the joint must be thoroughly cleaned, a suitable flux must be used, a filler metal (spelter) is used and heat is applied to the joint. However, in this case a much higher temperature is used (850°C to 900°C), making it necessary to use a naked flame (or an electric arc). Brazing is used in preference to soft soldering in applications where greater strength in the joint is required. Where in soft soldering the joint must be lapped, in brazing it may also be butt jointed. (Fig. 1.1.b). Brazing is not normally used for making electrical connections.

3.a. ii. 1 Fluxes and filler metals for brazing

- Flux – a compound of borax
- Filler metal – an alloy of copper and zinc (spelter)

3.a. ii. 2 Procedure

The procedure to be followed is fully described in the series book *Soft Soldering, Hard Soldering and Brazing* (Section 10). The following points are essential to that procedure:

- the surfaces to be joined must be cleaned
- the flame used must not be too fierce, *or*
- the carbon arc employed must be of a suitable size for the work.

3.a. ii. 3 Faults

A common fault is applying too hot a flame or arc which melts the parent metal and results in craters in the workpiece.

3.a. iii Safety

The use of naked flames and heat is always hazardous. Sensible precautions are therefore essential. In particular, the work should never be carried out near combustible materials, nor where flammable liquids or gases are present, e.g. petrol tanks.
The following precautions are specific to the method in use.

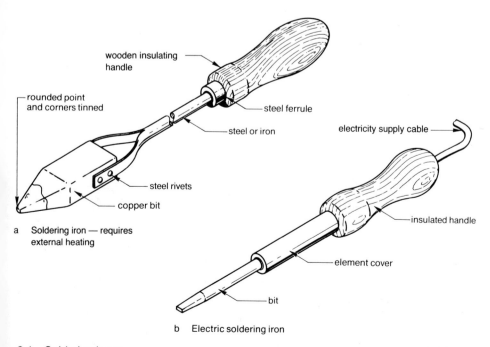

wooden insulating handle

rounded point and corners tinned

steel ferrule

steel or iron

electricity supply cable

steel rivets

copper bit

insulated handle

a   Soldering iron — requires external heating

element cover

bit

b   Electric soldering iron

3.1   Soldering irons

3.a. iii. 1 In soldering

- care must be taken to avoid burns
- when using a corrosive flux care must be taken to avoid any contact with the body, particularly with the eyes.

3.a. iii. 2 In brazing

- goggles must be worn to protect the eyes
- when a torch is in use, normal fire precautions must be taken
- care must be taken to avoid burns
  when an electric arc is in use, **glasses or head-shield with an ultra-violet filter lens must be worn**.

3.b Welding

Welding can be defined as: the joining of suitable metals, usually by raising the temperature at the joint so that the parts may be united by fusion or by forging or under pressure. The welding temperature may be attained by external heating, by passing an electric current through the joint or by striking an electric arc between an electrode (filler metal rod) and the components to be joined. During the welding process the metal at the point of contact between the components to be joined is melted and the components are fused together. To achieve this fusion in, for example, mild steel, very high temperatures are necessary (3800°C to 4300°C). Except in resistance spot welding a filler rod is used to supplement the fused metal and a flux is used to protect the molten metal (weld pool) from oxidation. Welding is used where great strength in the joint is required, e.g. large steel fabrications.

It is most important that safety precautions are observed. Protective gloves, goggles, helmet or hand-held shield must be used. When electric arc welding is being undertaken the arc must never be viewed by the naked eye. Precautions against the risk of fire must be taken.

3.b. i Gas welding

Gas welding is used extensively in 'on site' welding where mains electricity supplies are not available, e.g. agricultural engineering work. The most common of the gas welding procedures uses the oxy-acetylene mixture as the combustible source of heat. A mixture of oxygen and inflammable acetylene is ignited, the temperature of the flame being controlled by the proportions of oxygen and acetylene in the mix. Generally the more oxygen, the hotter the flame. However, if the percentage of oxygen is too high the acetylene will be burnt faster than it can be supplied and the flame will extinguish. (Fig. 3.2.)

3.b. ii Manual metal arc welding

In the manual metal arc welding process an electric arc is formed by the passage of an electric current between a flux-coated electrode and the workpiece (Fig. 3.3). The temperature of the arc is about 4300°C and is sufficient to cause the edges of the components to be joined to fuse together. The electrode itself melts and forms part of the welded joint, whilst the flux protects the weld pool (the molten metal at the point of fusion) from oxidation. Manual metal arc welding is replacing gas welding as the general-purpose welding procedure because of the widespread availability of a mains electricity supply and the development of lightweight portable electric generators. It is used extensively in the field of 'on site' fabrication, agricultural engineering, engineering workshops and various industrial situations.

3.b. iii Resistance spot welding

This process is used extensively for joining two pieces of sheet metal together. The principle employed is that when an electric current is caused to flow through a resistance, heat is generated. Consider Figs. 3.4 and 3.5. Two metal sheets to be joined are clamped together between copper electrodes. There are three contact points, R1, R2 and R3. Owing to the shape of the electrodes, they tend to press into the sheets at R1 and R2, so creating a very low contact resistance. At R3, however, the contact resistance between the two sheets is relatively high. A very high current (in the order of 100 000 amperes) is passed through the electrodes and the joining point of the metal sheets (R3). This current causes heat to be generated at the point of high resistance (R3). The heat is sufficient to cause the metal to fuse and complete the joint.

3.c Riveting

A rivet is a headed shank used for making a permanent joint between two or more pieces (Fig. 3.6). It is 'closed' by forming a head on the projecting part of the shank by hammering or other means. The head may be rounded, flat, pan-shaped or countersunk (Fig. 3.7).

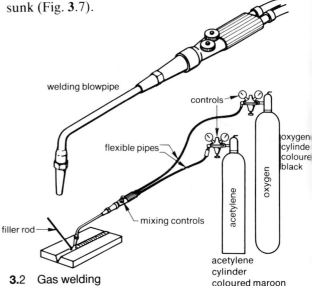

welding blowpipe

controls

flexible pipes

mixing controls

filler rod

oxygen cylinder coloured black

oxygen

acetylene

acetylene cylinder coloured maroon

3.2 Gas welding

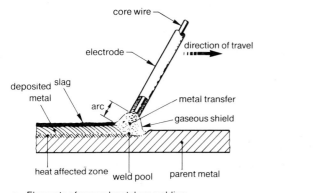

a   Elements of manual metal arc welding

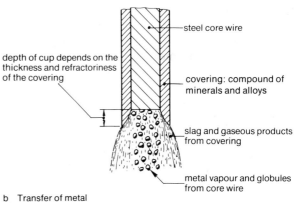

b   Transfer of metal

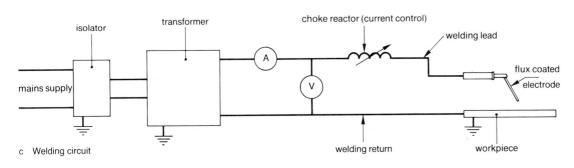

c   Welding circuit

3.3   Manual metal arc welding shown diagrammatically

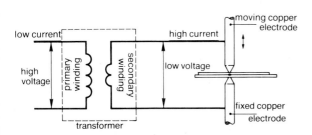

3.4   Resistance spot welding: line diagram

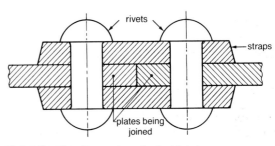

3.6   Section through a riveted joint

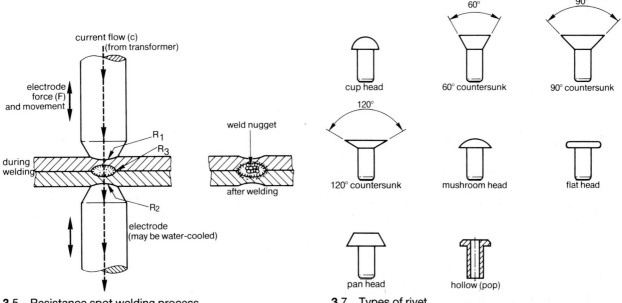

3.5   Resistance spot welding process

3.7   Types of rivet

14

Rivets are manufactured from various materials, low carbon steel, copper, brass and aluminium alloy and are produced in various sizes. They are used to join metal to metal, metal to fabric and to make patch repairs in sheet metal.

3.c. i Methods and tools used

As a general rule the riveting process is carried out either 'cold', i.e. at ambient temperature, when using soft metal rivets of up to 5 mm diameter or 'hot', i.e. at about 850°C for steel rivets of over 5 mm diameter. Heads are formed using specially shaped tools and a hand-held hammer for small rivets and those made from soft metals. Power-operated hammers are used for large rivets and those made from hard metals. Fig. 3.8 shows how, using hand tools only, a head is formed on a cup-head rivet joining two plates. The following tools are required:

- *Ball pein hammer* – to swell the rivet in the hole and to roughly shape the head
- *Drawing up tool* – to close the gap between the pieces to be joined
- *Rivet snap* – to shape the rivet head
- *Support dolly* – to support the rivet.

The same principle is used for large rivets and for hot riveting, but in this case power (often pneumatic) hammers of a size to suit the rivet are used.
Interchangeable snaps to suit the type of rivet head required are supplied with the power hammer.

3.c. ii 'Pop' riveting

'Pop' rivets are used in lightweight fabrications in the electrical and electronic industries and on panel work in the motor and aerospace industries. Their design enables them to be secured from one side of the work without the need for a supporting dolly. The use of 'pop' rivets calls for a different procedure. A 'pop' rivet has two parts:

- *The rivet*, which is hollow and is made from soft metal alloy or steel
- *The mandrel*, made from steel

The method of securing a 'pop' rivet is shown in Fig. 3.9. The rivet is placed in the holes drilled in the material to be joined and the riveting pliers (Fig. 3.9a) are applied to the protruding mandrel.
Gripping the pliers tightly causes the mandrel to be drawn up, so compressing the soft metal of the rivet before, under continuing pressure, the mandrel snaps at the neck (Fig. 3.9c). The joint is then secure (Fig. 3.9d).

3.c. iii Riveted joint proportions

The configuration of a riveted joint, type and spacing of the rivets, is normally specified by the fabrication designer. However as a guide to good practice Fig. 3.10 is included to illustrate typical riveted joints. Dimensions are given in terms of the shank diameter (dia) of the rivet.

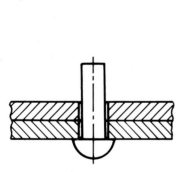

a   Rivet placed in hole

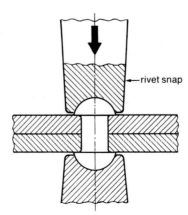

b   Support dolly and drawing up tool in place

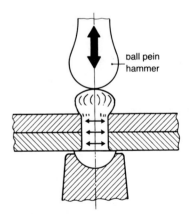

c   Rivet struck squarely to swell it in hole.

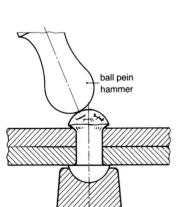

d   Roughly forming rivet head

e   Rivet head finally shaped with a rivet snap

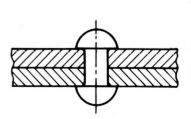

f   Completed riveted joint

3.8   Making a riveting joint: sequence

3.c. iv Typical faults in riveted joints

Fig. **3**.11 illustrates faults that may occur in riveted joints. A brief note indicating the cause of each fault is included with the illustration. Many of the faults will be prevented if the rivets used are of the correct size and the components to be joined are clamped together whilst the rivet holes are drilled and until the first rivet is secured.

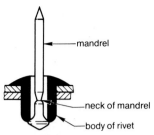

b   Rivet in place

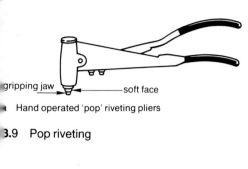

a   Hand operated 'pop' riveting pliers

3.9   Pop riveting

c   Action of riveting pliers

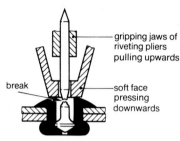

d   Completed joint

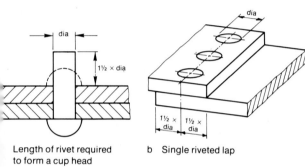

Length of rivet required to form a cup head

b   Single riveted lap

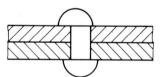

a   Rivet set struck off centre

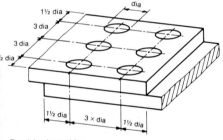

Double riveted lap

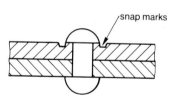

b   Rivet too long

Single strap butt

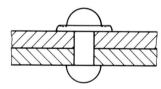

c   Rivet too short

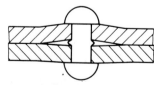

Double strap butt

d   Rivet not drawn up

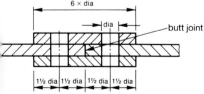

Joggled lap

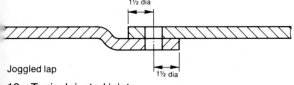

3.10   Typical riveted joints

e   Hole too large, rivet diameter too small

3.11   Faults in riveted joints

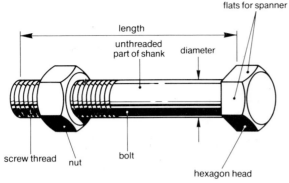

3.12   Hexagonal head nut and bolt

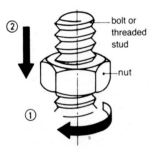

Note: A flat washer is placed between the nut (and sometimes the bolt head) and the material in order to distribute pressure.

3.13   Torque and clamping force: bolted joint

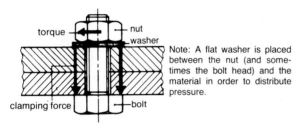

① rotation of nut
② linear movement of nut

3.14   Conversion of motion by screw thread

3.d Joining by bolt and screw

The construction of a bolt is shown in Fig. **3.**12. Together with a nut it affords the most common means of joining two components (Figs. **3.**13 and **3.**16b). In some applications a screw/bolt is used without a nut, when one of the parts to be joined is drilled and tapped to accept the screw thread (Fig. **3.**16a).

The function of a screw thread is to enable rotary motion to be converted to linear motion (Fig. **3.**14). This action pulls together the components to be secured. There is no real difference between a screw (excluding wood screws) and a bolt, but generally the term bolt is applied when a spanner is necessary for tightening (or loosening) and the term screw is applied when a screwdriver is necessary. In some instances both spanner and/or screwdriver can be used. Generally a bolt is used in heavier applications. Bolts, screws and nuts are made in a great many sizes and from many materials, steels, steel alloys, non-ferrous metals and from non-metals such as nylon. Bolts and screws are identified by:

- shank diameter
- type of screw thread
- length
- material
- shape of head.

The type of bolt or screw to be used is determined by the application, e.g.:

- *The choice of diameter* is usually a reflection of the mechanical strength required.
- *The choice of screw thread* is important. As a general rule it can be stated that a coarse thread is used if the material into which the screw is to be secured is soft, e.g. copper, aluminium, nylon, or is coarse-grained as is cast iron. A fine thread is used where a harder material is to accept the screw, e.g. steel, bronze.
- *The choice of screw length* is determined by the distance to be spanned to effect a secure joint.

Table 3.2. Screw/bolt material related to requirement

Requirement	Material
Normal duties – medium strength	– Mild steel
High strength	– High tensile (capable of being stretched) steel
Lightweight	– Light alloy
Corrosive conditions, high strength	– Stainless steel
Corrosive conditions, medium strength	– Plated mild steel
Corrosive conditions, lightweight	– Nylon/other plastic
For use in an environment where there are large variations in temperatures	– With similar coefficient of expansion consistent with the requirements of strength

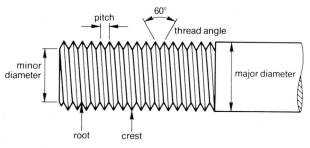

3.15 Screw thread

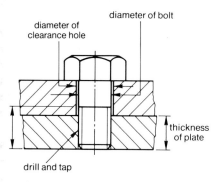

a A bolt fitted into a tapped hole to complete a joint

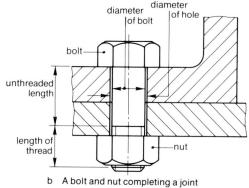

b A bolt and nut completing a joint

3.16 Joining by screw thread

- *The choice of material* is generally determined by the duty to be performed and the environment in which it is to be used. Table 3.2 lists some requirements and the appropriate choices of bolt/screw material. It is essential that if a damaged bolt/screw is replaced, the replacement should have the same material specification.
Note: A further consideration must be cost; the use of high tensile steel, stainless steel and light alloy bolts is more costly than, for example, mild steel and the designer will weigh the cost against the particular engineering requirements and reach a decision accordingly.
- *The choice of head* is determined by design considerations. If, for example, it is required that the surface of the component, through which the screw is to be passed to secure a component, should be free of obstructions then a countersunk-headed screw might be the choice.

3.d. i Forms of screw thread

In 1963 screw threads were standardised by the International Standards Organisation (ISO). Before that date there were several forms of screw thread in use. In Britain the most common forms were:

- British Standard Whitworth (BSW) — V thread. Angle 55°
- British Standard Fine (BSF) — V thread. Angle dependent on diameter
- British Association (BA) — V thread. Angle 47½°
- British Standard Pipe (BSP) — V thread. Angle 55°

The ISO metric screw thread system is detailed in BS 3643; it has a V thread form with a 60° included angle (Fig. **3.**15).

ISO standard screws are available with both coarse and fine threads. Where a screw is designated, for example M6 × 0.75, the screw will have a diameter of 6 mm and a fine thread of 0.75 pitch; if, however, the designation is M6 only, the screw will have a diameter of 6 mm and a coarse thread.

Screw threads are generally right-handed, i.e. the thread is cut in such a way that a clockwise rotation is needed in order to tighten the screw in the nut or seating. However, in some applications a left-hand thread is required, and in that case a counter-clockwise rotation will be needed to tighten the screw. An example of this application can be found on the rotating components of many machines where the rotation is such that a right-hand threaded screw would be loosened.

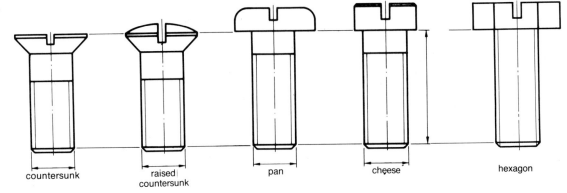

3.17   Screw head profiles

3.d. ii Types of bolts and screws

Fig. **3**.12 details the names given to the parts of a hexagonal headed nut and bolt.
Screws are produced with a variety of heads (Fig. **3**.17):
- countersunk head
- instrument head (raised countersunk)
- pan head
- cheese head
- hexagon head.

The heads of the screws are machined to suit the type of screwdriver to be used; the most common are shown in Fig. **3**.18:
- *Slotted head:* the most common type in use. It has the disadvantage that the screwdriver blade can easily distort the screw slot and can slip from the slot and score the surface of the component into which the screw is being secured.
- *Cross head:* this type of head is becoming more popular and will perhaps replace the slotted head type. The design is such that the screwdriver is less likely to slip. The Philips head screw is a type of crosshead screw.
- *Socket head:* also known as the Allen screw, it is tightened with a wrench (Allen key); this allows the screw to be tightened to a greater degree than is the case with a slotted or cross head type of screw.

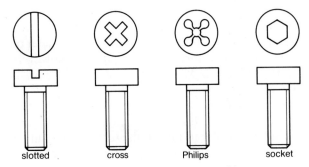

3.18   Types of screw heads to suit screwdrivers

3.d. iii Studs

If a bolt is repeatedly removed from the tapped hole in a component, there will be wear on the screw threads in the component and the component may need to be replaced. If a threaded stud is screwed into the component and a nut is used to secure the

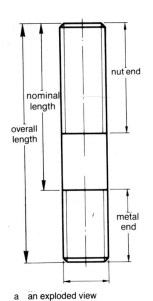

a   an exploded view

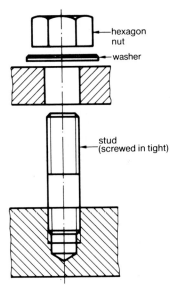

b   joining using a screwed stud

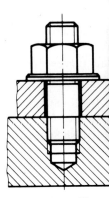

c   detail of assembly

3.19   Screwed stud

other component to be joined, then during dismantling/assembling any wear will be confined to the easily and cheaply replaced stud (Fig. **3.**19), e.g. the studs securing the cylinder head to the engine block of a car.

Studs are also used where access is difficult, e.g. the studs securing water pumps to car engines.

3.d. iv Screw threads for pipe joints

Screw threads are used extensively for securing joints in pipes which convey substances such as water, oil, gas and steam, or for a protective conduit for electricity cables. A simple screwed pipe joint is shown in Fig. **3.**20.

3.d. v 4 *Spring washer*
Made from hardened steel, this washer is formed as a single (sometimes double) coil helix. The washer is compressed when the nut is tightened. Any tendency to loosen under vibration is prevented by the hard steel biting into the nut, thereby preventing rotation (Fig. **3.**24).

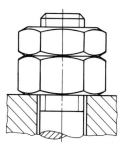

3.21 Use of a lock nut

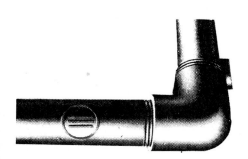

3.20 A simple screwed pipe joint

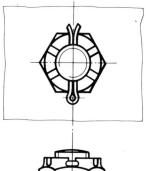
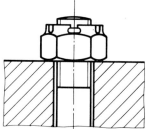

3.22 Slotted castle nut and split pin

3.d. v Locking devices

It is often necessary to lock nuts on to screws, bolts or studs to prevent them being loosened by vibration. A variety of locking devices is available.

3.d. v 1 *Lock nut*
This comprises two nuts screwed firmly one on top of the other. The effect is that the nut threads wedge against the opposite flanks of the bolt thread, thus giving a locking effect (Fig. **3.**21).

3.d. v 2 *Slotted castle nut*
In this system the nut is castellated and a pin (split pin, see Section 3. h. i) is passed through the castellations and the shank of the bolt, effectively preventing further movement of the nut (Fig. **3.**22).

3.d. v 3 *Self-locking nut*
Self-locking nuts contain a fibre or nylon insert (Fig. **3.**23). As the nut is turned on the screw thread the insert is deformed. There is high friction between the threaded shaft and the insert. This friction prevents the nut from being loosened by vibration. The self-locking property is lost when this type of nut is used more than once.

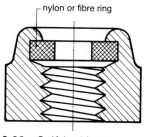

3.23 Self-locking nut

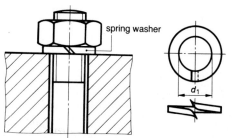

3.24 Spring washer

3.d. v 5 Serrated (shakeproof) washer

A serrated washer is a ring washer with projections around the circumference (Fig. 3.25). It functions in much the same way as the spring washer.

Warning: Many shakeproof washers contain beryllium oxide. They must not be filed or machined. The particles released are highly toxic.

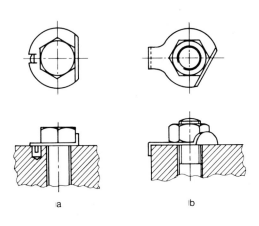

a   b

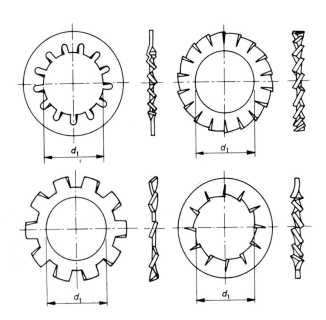

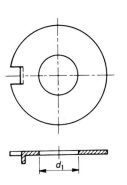

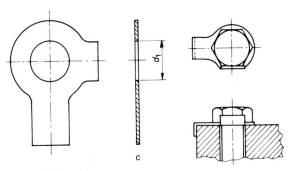

c

3.26   Tab washers

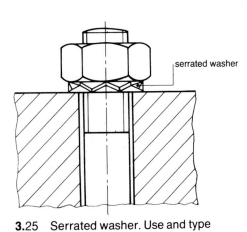

serrated washer

3.25   Serrated washer. Use and type

3.d. v 6 Tab washer

These are placed between the nut and the face of the component (Fig. 3.26c). One end is bent against the nut (Fig. 3.26b), the other is folded over the edge of the component or into a slot machined in the component (Fig. 3.26a).

3.e Adhesive bonding

Adhesives provide a permanent joining medium for many materials. They range from wallpaper pastes to high performance adhesives used in industry. Adhesives are classified in BS 5407. Of interest here are those adhesives used instead of welds, screws, bolts or rivets in industry. The use of adhesives in industry is well established. In the aircraft industry they are widely used; indeed the airframe of the Mosquito aircraft, a World War II fighter bomber, was constructed of wood joined with adhesives. The particular adhesive used had a bond strength greater than the wood itself. Today, adhesives are produced with a bond strength ten times stronger than that of the adhesive used in the Mosquito aircraft. A number of joints made by the use of adhesives are shown in Fig. 3.27.

3.e. i Purpose and application

Adhesives are used to join two or more components. The components joined may be made from a wide variety of materials. The variation of material determines the type of adhesive used. Adhesives are available for joining different combinations of materials:
- rubber to steel
- glass to plastic
- plastic to steel, etc.

In every case the preparation of the joint is most important, particularly where the joints are to be made between coated materials, e.g. galvanised or copper-coated sheets.

It it important to realise that there is no single adhesive which has the property of adhering to *all* materials and meeting *all* technical requirements.

Before any adhesive is used it is necessary to read and then follow the manufacturer's instructions carefully.

Warning: The vapour given off by many adhesives is toxic. When using adhesives great care must be taken to ensure that there is adequate ventilation.

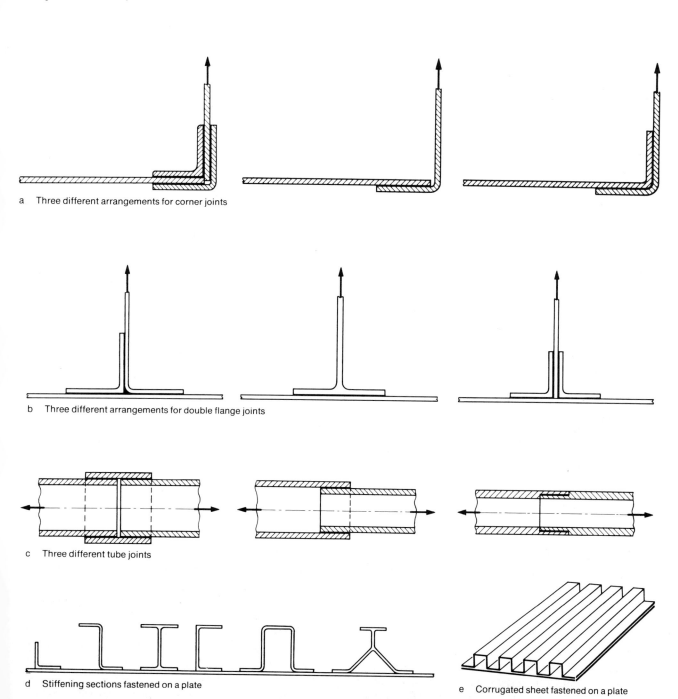

a   Three different arrangements for corner joints

b   Three different arrangements for double flange joints

c   Three different tube joints

d   Stiffening sections fastened on a plate

e   Corrugated sheet fastened on a plate

3.27   Adhesive joints

3.e. ii Forms of supply

Whilst adhesives are best known by their trade
names, all adhesives may be classified into two main
categories: natural and synthetic. Fig. **3.**28 shows
some of the packaging and presentation of adhesives.

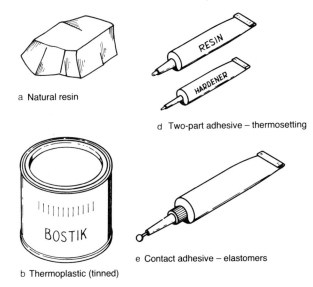

a Natural resin

d Two-part adhesive – thermosetting

3.e. ii 1 Natural adhesives
Natural adhesives are manufactured from combinations of animal and vegetable protein, often with
minerals such as sodium silicate added. They are used
extensively in the construction, woodworking, soft
furnishing, fancy goods and decoration industries. As
a general rule natural adhesives form strong joints
when dry but they are susceptible to extremes of
temperature and humidity.

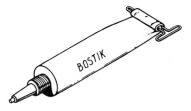

b Thermoplastic (tinned)

e Contact adhesive – elastomers

3.e. ii 2 Synthetic adhesives
Synthetic adhesives may be further categorised into:
- Thermosetting resins
- Thermoplastic resins
- Elastomers (thermoplastic rubbers).

c Thermoplastic (tubed)

3.28   Packaging and presentation of adhesives

3.e. ii 2 a. **Thermosetting resins:** These are the
common two-part adhesives, with a resin and a
hardener. Kept separate, the parts are chemically
inactive but when they are mixed a chemical reaction
takes place which causes the mixture to harden. This
property is made use of when making a joint. Pressure and a slight rise in temperature will usually assist
the hardening process. Joints made with thermosetting resins are not readily affected by changes in
temperature, humidity and chemical reactions; they
usually have a high bond strength but the joints tend
to be brittle. The main application of this type of
adhesive is to join metals, concrete, glass and plastics.

3.e. ii 2 b. **Thermoplastic resins:** These are usually
one-part in either liquid or solid form. The liquid
form is supplied in containers and is ready for use.
The solid form must be melted before use. Pressure
must be applied when joining with thermoplastic
resins but it is not necessary to apply heat. The bond
strength is less than that of thermosetting resins, but
the joint is less brittle. Their main uses are for bonding glass, rubber, plastics and wood. Thermoplastic
resins may be further sub-divided into two main
groups:
- *Acrylics* – these are quick-drying and are used to
  bond materials such as glass, perspex and wood.
  Acrylics have the advantage of being waterproof.
- *Cellulose* – these are quick-drying, they resist the
  entry of water, but are weak when subjected to
  tensile loads. These resins are used for bonding
  natural fabrics, leather and paper.

3.e. ii 2 c. **Elastomers (thermoplastic rubbers):**
These are contact adhesives; they contain a solvent
that, when exposed to air, evaporates. These adhesives are normally applied to both surfaces to be
joined, left for a short time until they become 'tacky'
and then the joint is made by pressing the surfaces
together to expel any air. Elastomers are used to join
rubber, plastics and laminates.
Included in this category are the **cyanoacrylate** adhesives, commonly called **'super glues'**. These are very
quick-acting adhesives and are used extensively for
the assembly of small electrical and electronic components.

3.e. iii Methods used

The effectiveness of an adhesive bond is dependent
on:
- the composition of the adhesives
- the effect of the adhesive on the materials being
  joined
- the effect of the materials being joined on the
  adhesive
- the effect of the atmosphere on both the adhesive
  and the joint
- the effect of temperature on both the adhesive
  and the joint
- a combination of all the above.
Manufacturers' instructions include notes relating to
the factors listed above, together with any special
requirements such as:
- the surface texture of the components to be joined
- the shape of the parts in the area of the joint

- the cleanliness of the surfaces being joined; they should be dry and free of dirt, grease and corrosion.
- the time for a bond to harden or 'cure'
- the application of clamps or other means of exerting pressure.

The instructions must be followed to ensure that effective joints are achieved. Except where repetitive or large-scale production requirements have to be met, very little equipment is required to make effective joints. Usually all that is needed is a spreader to ensure even distribution of the adhesive.

3.e. iv Precautions to be observed

It is most important to remember that toxic or flammable fumes are released by some adhesives. It is essential to take the appropriate safety precautions. These include:
- ensuring good ventilation of the working area
- not smoking or using naked flames in the work area
- using protective clothing such as gloves and masks
- using a barrier cream on the hands.

You should always wash thoroughly after using adhesives.

3.f Shrunk joints

That property of a metal that causes it to expand when heated and contract when cooled is used in this process of making joints. Shrunk joints are used to make a bond between two or more components. The joint is temporary in that the bond can be broken when further heat is applied. However, the application of even heating, which is often required, is sometimes difficult to achieve outside a controlled environment. No additional fastenings, e.g. bolts, screws, rivets or joining materials are needed. There are two categories of shrunk joint:
- hot shrunk joints
- cold shrunk joints.

3.f. i Hot shrunk joints

Let us suppose that a ring is to be placed and secured onto a shaft and that the internal diameter of the ring is slightly less than the diameter of the shaft. If the ring is heated it will expand and the internal diameter will increase, making it possible to draw the ring over the shaft and place it in the required position. As the ring cools, it contracts and grips the shaft and so secures the joint (Fig. **3.**29).

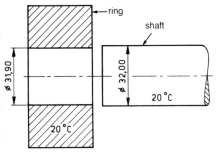

a Shaft and ring to be joined

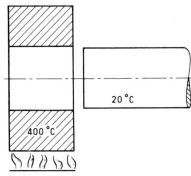

b Heat being applied to the ring

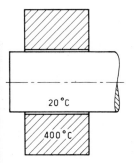

c Ring expanded and drawn over shaft

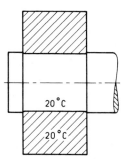

d Ring cools and grips shaft. Joint completed.

3.29 Hot shrinking

3.f. ii Cold shrunk joints

The same principle as is used in hot shrunk joints is used in cold shrinking.

Suppose a bush is to be secured in an engine block (Fig. 3.30), but the diameter of the bush is slightly larger than the diameter of the bush seating in the engine block. If the bush is cooled, the diameter will shrink until it becomes possible to fit the bush into the block. As the temperature of the bush rises to that of the block, it expands and is held firmly in place.

3.f. iii Applications

Shrunk joints are used for the following reasons:
● to save identical material – Fig. **3**.31
● to save expensive material – Fig. **3**.32
● to save production costs – Fig. **3**.33
● to facilitate the use of different materials for differing purposes – Figs. **3**.32 and **3**.34.

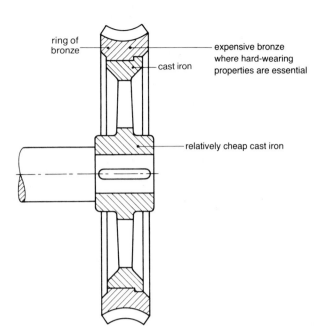

3.32   Wormwheel with cast iron body and a bronze ring

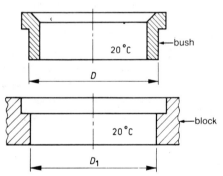

a   Bush and block to be joined

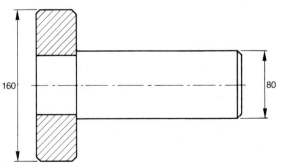

b   Bush shrunk as a result of cooling

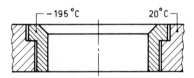

c   Bush now fits into block

d   Bush expands and is held securely. Joint completed

3.30   Cold shrinking

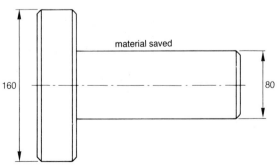

a   'Shaded area illustrates wastage of material if machined from a solid shaft of 160 diameter

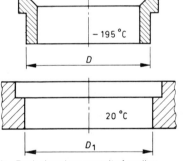

b   collar shrunk on a shaft of 80 diameter: shaft and collar

3.31   Saving material by shrinking: shaft and collar

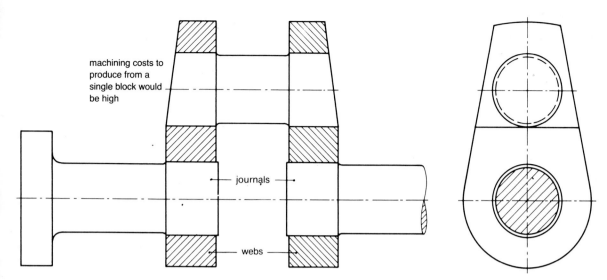

3.33 Crankshaft with webs shrunk on to journals

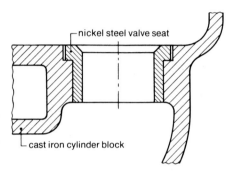

3.34 Valve seat shrunk into cylinder block

3.f. iv Procedure

The procedure for making shrunk joints may be carried out in four stages:
- manufacturing components to the appropriate form, finish and accuracy
- heating and/or cooling
- assembly
- completing the joint by allowing components to reach the same temperature.

3.f. iv 1 Manufacture
The mating components must be manufactured to the design specification.

3.f. iv 2 Heating and/or cooling
It is important that during the heating/cooling process, protective clothing, e.g. overalls, gloves, etc. is worn by operators. Tongs, wire mesh baskets or where necessary specially designed lifting equipment, must be used for the transportation of the very hot or very cold components.

As a general rule it is more economical to heat a component than to cool it.

For most materials used for shrunk joints it is practicable to raise the temperature to 400°C, whereas cooling is limited to about −190°C.

To avoid excessive heating and cooling of mating components it is sometimes more convenient to heat one component and cool the other, e.g. a shaft could be cooled to −150°C whilst the mating collar was heated to +150°C, thus giving a temperature difference of 300°C.

3.f. v Assembly

When shrunk joints are made the difference in the diameters of their mating surfaces is small. On assembly, as the hot/cold component makes contact with the mating component, there is a rapid exchange of heat and the components quickly reach the same temperature. It is therefore essential that during assembly the components are quickly located in their correct position. Failure to work quickly and accurately results in incorrect positioning.

3.f. vi Everyday use of the principle

Removing the metal screw cap from a glass container can be a difficult task; however, if the container cap and neck are immersed in warm water the metal screw cap expands rather more than the glass and may be unscrewed with little effort.

3.g Compression joints

The purpose of the compression joint is to make a secure bond between two components at the same temperature without the use of additional fastenings.

26

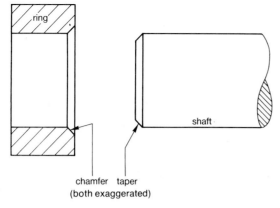

3.35 Centring edge

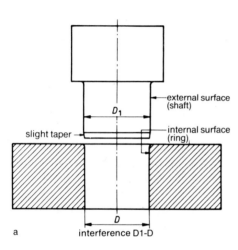

a

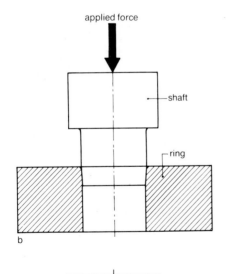

b

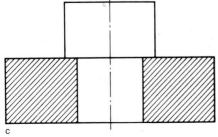

c

3.36 Making a compression joint: sequence

3.g. i Terms used

The following terms are used in the explanation of a compression joint:

- *shaft* – external mating surface
- *ring* – internal mating surface
- *interference* – the difference in the mating dimensions of the shaft and ring before compression
- *centring edge* – either a slight taper on the leading edge of the shaft, or a slight chamfer formed on the leading edge of the ring (Fig. **3**.35). The centring edge assists in centring the ring on the shaft before pressure is applied.

Notes:
1 To form a compression joint the diameter of the shaft is always greater than the diameter of the ring.
2 It is the amount of interference that determines the type of joint formed. If the interference is large, a large force will be required to assemble the ring on to the shaft; this might lead to damage. If the interference is small, a smaller force will be required for assembly but in service the joint may be insecure. Grades of interference are specified in BS 4500.

3.g. ii Procedure

Fig. **3**.36 shows the sequence of operations carried out when making a compression joint. They are summarised below:
- Manufacture the shaft and ring to the design specification.
- Clean the surface to be joined.
- Apply a lubricant to the mating surfaces. The lubricant reduces friction and will minimise the effect of 'digging in' on assembly. The lubricant will also aid dismantling if this becomes necessary.
- Locate the ring and shaft in the correct positions relative to each other. (Fig. **3**.37 shows an incorrect method of compression fitting a ball race.)
- Press the ring and shaft together.

Specified procedures should be followed closely, since some materials are more suited to being subjected to compression rather than tension.

Examples of methods used for making compression joints are shown in Fig. **3**.38 and Fig. **3**.39.
- Fig. **3**.38 shows how a bush may be drawn into a hole by using a stud between two washers.
- Fig **3**.39 shows ball races being fitted:
  a. in a housing by pressing or careful tapping on a piece of piping held in contact with the outer race.
  b. on a shaft by pressure or careful tapping by a piece of piping held in contact with the inner race.

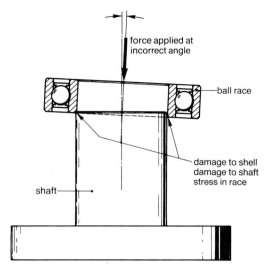

3.37 Incorrect alignment or incorrect application of force leads to damage

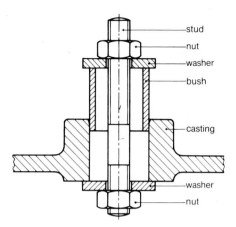

3.38 Securing a bush into a casting

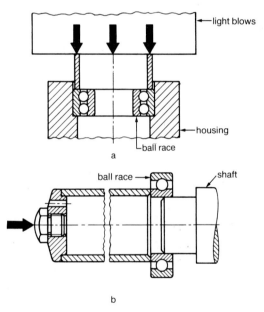

3.39 Mounting a ball race

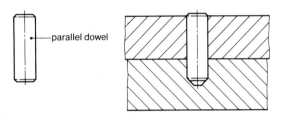

3.40 Plain (parallel) dowel

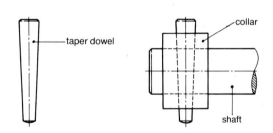

3.41 Tapered dowel

3.h Pins and keys

Pins and keys provide temporary joints and establish precise location between two components.

3.h. i Pins

Pins are divided into several categories:
- **Parallel shank pin** – also termed a 'dowel' – this fits into a precisely reamed hole. It is mostly used to establish the precise location of two components relative to each other (Fig. **3**.40).
  Note: The holes do not always extend through both components.
- **Taper pin** – this fits into a precisely reamed hole which has the same taper and is used to attach pulleys, collars and wheels on to shafts, (Fig. **3**.41). A tapered pin is used in preference to a parallel pin for the following reasons:
  a. A taper pin can be used for precisely locating

into a shaft. A parallel pin may permit two components to be assembled 180° out of alignment. (Fig. **3**.42).

b. A taper pin can only be removed by the same route as it entered the work. In some cases a parallel pin can be pushed right through.

c. A taper pin normally establishes a firmer joint.

• **Cotter pin** – a cotter pin can be described as being a parallel pin with, at one end, a threaded stud of smaller diameter than the pin shaft and with a flattened tapered panel on one portion of the plain shaft (Fig. **3.**43). The cotter pin is used to locate a collar on a shaft and is secured in place by means of a nut and washer on the threaded stud. A typical use is securing a bicycle pedal crank to its shaft.

• **Split pin** – a split pin is used solely as a securing device. It consists of a folded over, half round section strip of malleable metal. Placed through a drilled hole, the protruding free ends are opened to secure it in place. Split pins are not required to transmit driving forces as are taper and cotter pins. Typical uses are as a locking pin to prevent the rotation of a nut or as a device to prevent lateral movement along a shaft (Fig. **3**.44).

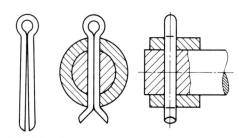
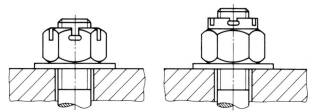

a   Split pin locating a ring on a shaft

b   Split pins securing castle and slotted nuts

3.44   Split pin use

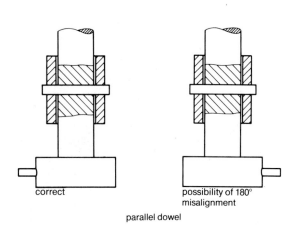

correct — possibility of 180° misalignment — parallel dowel

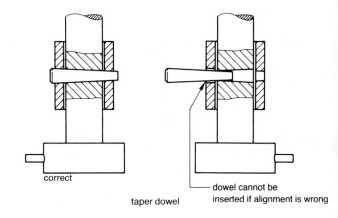

correct — taper dowel — dowel cannot be inserted if alignment is wrong

3.42   Advantage of taper over parallel pin

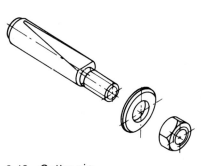
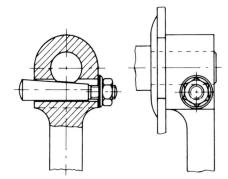

3.43   Cotter pin

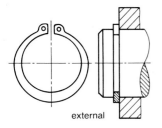

external

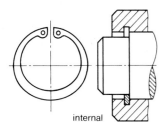

internal

3.45   Circlips

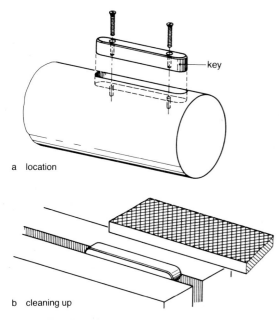

a   location

b   cleaning up

3.46   Feather (flat) key

3.h. ii Circlips

Circlips are made of spring steel and are used to provide a locating shoulder on a shaft (external) or in a hole (internal) (Fig. **3.**45). Circlips are sprung into place by using specially shaped pliers.

3.h. iii Keys

Keys are located between a wheel and a shaft in order to transmit power. They prevent rotation of a shaft and wheel relative to each other. There are three main types of key in common use:
- Feather (flat) key (Fig. **3.**46) – These keys are fixed to the shaft and are termed permanent keys.
- Gib head (taper) key (Fig. **3.**47) – These keys are termed loose keys and are inserted into the keyway after the component is assembled on the shaft. The key protrudes and is easily accessible for dismantling purposes.
- Woodruff key (Fig. **3.**48) – These are termed loose keys and are inserted into the shaft keyway before assembly. They are not accessible for dismantling purposes until the shaft and component are separated.

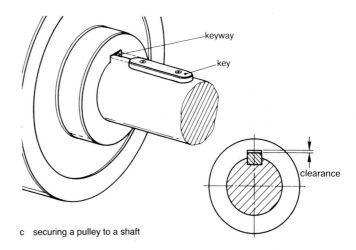

c   securing a pulley to a shaft

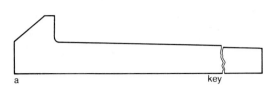

a   key

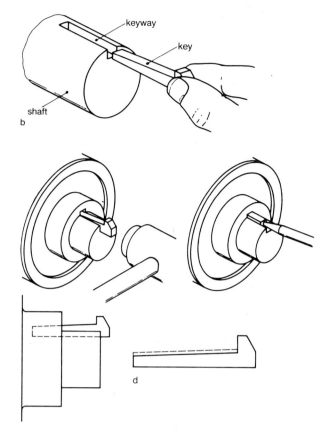

keyway

key

shaft

b

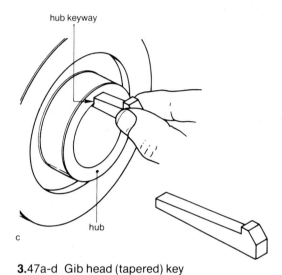

hub keyway

hub

c

3.47a-d Gib head (tapered) key

d

All keys must be fitted carefully. Points to note are:
- they must be of the correct size
- they must be free from corrosion
- they must be free from burrs; Fig. **3.**46a illustrates a feather key being cleared of burrs with a file

- the hub and keyway must be clean and free from burrs
- they must fit securely in place with no lateral movement between the shaft and the hub.

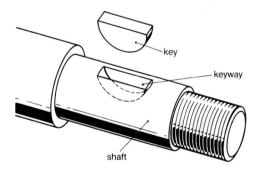

key

keyway

shaft

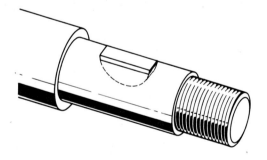

3.48 Woodruff key

4 Equipment and consumables

Table 4.1 gives a summary of the equipment and consumables used in the various joining processes discussed in this book. The reference numbers of some useful related illustrations are given in the right-hand column of the table.

Table 4.1 Summary of equipment and consumables used in joining

Ref	Joining process	Equipment and consumables used or source references	Relevant Fig. Nos.
4a and 4b	Soldering, oxy-fuel welding and brazing	Heat sources: Open flame burner for hand-held irons Electricity supply Oxygen and acetylene (gas cylinders) Solders, filler rod and fluxes: Soft solders; stick and resin cored Filler metal; specifications BS 1845 Filler rod; specifications BS 1453 Fluxes; zinc chloride, fluxite and borax type	**4**.1 and **4**.2
4c and 4d	Manual metal arc welding	Heat sources: Electricity supply; mains and portable generators Transformers and transformer rectifiers Safety equipment: Protective clothing; helmet, goggles, hand-held shields and gloves Equipment: Cables, return clamps and electrode holders Electrodes: Specifications listed in BS 639	**4**.3, **4**.4 and **4**.5
4e and 4f	Riveting	Riveting equipment Rivet set; support dolly, rivet snaps ball pein hammer and drawing up tool 'Pop' riveting pliers Pneumatic riveting hammer Rivets Classified by shape of head, cup mushroom, countersunk (60°, 90°, 120°) flat, pan and hollow ('pop')	**4**.6, **3**.7 **3**.9

Table 4.1   contd/.

32

Ref	Joining process	Equipment and consumables used or source references	Relevant Fig. Nos.
4g	Joining by screw thread	Bolts, screws, studs and nuts: Classified by thread, diameter, length material and head shape (refer to Section 3.d)	**3.**12
4h	Joining by pins, dowels and keys	Pins: Taper, cotter and split pins	**3.**43
		Dowels: Parallel shaft pins. Taper dowels	
		Keys: Feather, gib head and woodruff key	**3.**46, **3.**47 and **3.**48
4i	Joining by adhesives	Natural adhesives Various combinations of animal and vegetable protein	
		Synthetic adhesives: Thermosetting resins, thermoplastic resins, elastomers (thermoplastic rubbers)	
4j	Joining by shrinking	Heating equipment: Forge type furnaces, gas flame, electric elements, oil or gas fired furnaces and hot oil baths	
		Cooling equipment: Liquid salt baths and CO_2 (dry ice)	
		Handling equipment: Tongs, baskets	
4k	Joining by compression	Presses: Bench mounted, floor mounted, hydraulically and hand (mechanically) operated Hand tools	**4.**7

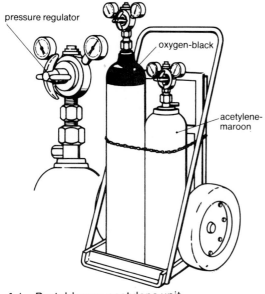

4.1   Portable oxy-acetylene unit

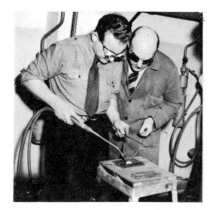

4.2   Welders' protective devices

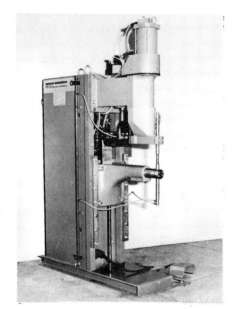

4.3   Air operated spot welding machine

4.4   Transformer rectifier

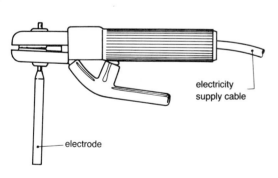

electricity
supply cable

electrode

4.5   Electrode holder and electrode

flux coating

core
wire

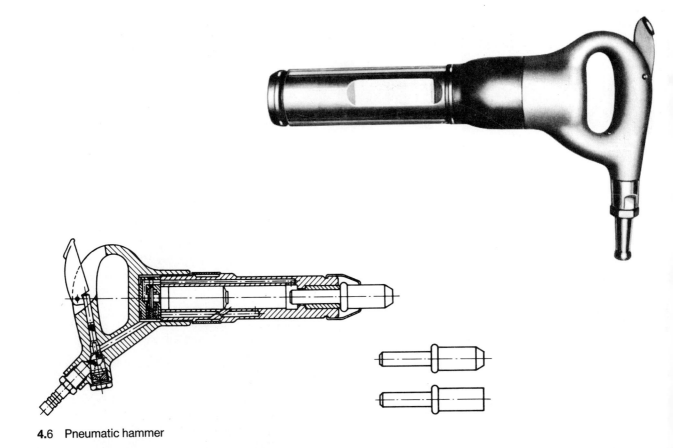

4.6   Pneumatic hammer

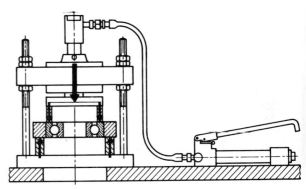

a.   Hand operated press

b   Hydraulically operated press

4.7   Presses

Technology of Skilled Processes

Basic Engineering Competences 201

Joining

Practice and test questions

**Published as a
co-operative venture
between
Stam Press Ltd**

and
City and Guilds

Practice and test questions

The questions in this book are intended to help the student achieve and demonstrate a knowledge and under-standing of the subject matter covered by this book. Accordingly, the questions follow the original section order, under the same headings. Finally there are questions spanning the sections and approximating to the level of those in the relevant examination of the City and Guilds of London Institute.

First published in Great Britain 1987
as a co-operative venture between Stam Press Ltd. and the City and Guilds of London Institute

© Stam Press Ltd. Cheltenham, 1987

Reprinted 1988

Printed and bound in Great Britain
by Martin's of Berwick.

1 and 2 Purpose of joining and range of joints

The following questions relate to the above aspects of joining, but what is stated here about answering them also applies to similarly framed questions covering later subject headings.

Many questions, as in the example below, provide a number of possible answers, usually four, lettered a, b, c and d. Only *one* is correct and you are required to decide which it is and circle the appropriate letter or number.

Example

Indicate which of the following joining processes can best be described as having the properties of both a temporary and a permanent joint.

a welding
b riveting
c joining by nut and bolt
d soft soldering

Where a written answer is required, this should be short and clear; where a sketch or diagram is required, this should be clear and adequately labelled.

---

1 When temporary joints are made the parts to be joined may be:
   a riveted
   b brazed
   c silver soldered
   d bolted

---

2 When a permanent joint is made the parts to be joined may be:
   a screwed
   b bolted
   c riveted
   d pinned

---

3 An assembly requires that two sheets of metal each 0.5 mm thick are joined together using a single lap joint. The sheets are to be well insulated from each other. To achieve this they should be joined together:
   a by welding
   b by riveting
   c with an impact adhesive
   d with an epoxy resin bond

---

4 The type of joint likely to fail first with increasing temperature will be one which is:
   a silver soldered
   b soft soldered
   c brazed
   d welded

---

5 The type of joint illustrated in the sketch is:
   a welded
   b soldered
   c brazed
   d using adhesives

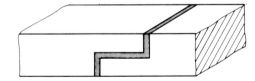

---

6 The joining process which results in the fusion of the parent metal is:
   a soldering
   b brazing
   c welding
   d riveting

---

7 Show by means of a sketch ONE application of a flexible joint.

3.a Soldering

The following questions relate to aspects of soldering. The correct answers should be given as explained on page 37.

---

1 State the main difference between soft soldering and brazing.

---

2 The element used with lead as the main constituent of a soft solder is:
   a silver
   b tin
   c copper
   d iron

---

3 The melting point of soft solders is generally between:
   a 100°C and 160°C
   b 183°C and 255°C
   c 240°C and 305°C
   d 850°C and 900°C

---

4 State what is meant by the solidification range of a solder.

---

5 State the circumstances in which the liquid flux zinc chloride should NOT be used in the soldering process.

---

6 The tip of a soldering iron must be coated with solder before an effective joint can be made. This process is known as:
   a wiping
   b dipping
   c fluxing
   d tinning

---

7 State why it is necessary to use a flux when soldering.

---

8 Give THREE causes of a dry joint.

---

9 Explain the procedure for preparing a brazed joint.

---

10 The filler metal used in the brazing process is an alloy of:
   a copper and zinc
   b lead and copper
   c copper and tin
   d zinc and lead

---

11 State the temperature range usually associated with the brazing process.

———————————————————————————
———————————————————————————

12 State TWO methods used to generate the heat required for brazing.

———————————————————————————
———————————————————————————
———————————————————————————
———————————————————————————

13 State the type of filters used in glasses and head-shields that protect the eyes during carbon arc brazing.

———————————————————————————
———————————————————————————
———————————————————————————
———————————————————————————

3.b Welding

The following questions relate to aspects of welding. The correct answers should be given as explained on page 37.

1 A combustible source of heat in the oxy-fuel gas welding process is usually:
   a nitrogen and acetylene
   b hydrogen and acetylene
   c oxygen and acetylene
   d nitrogen and oxygen

2 The approximate temperature of the arc used in the arc welding process is:
   a 1500°C
   b 3500°C
   c 4300°C
   d 5800°C

3 The purpose of using a flux in the welding process is to protect the weld pool from:
   a oxidation
   b cooling too quickly
   c flowing away from the joint area
   d contamination by the parent metal

4 State what is meant by the term 'fuse together' with reference to the welding of two components.

———————————————————————————
———————————————————————————
———————————————————————————

5 Describe, with the aid of a sketch, the process of resistance spot welding.

———————————————————————————
———————————————————————————
———————————————————————————
———————————————————————————
———————————————————————————
———————————————————————————
———————————————————————————

3.c Riveting

The following questions relate to aspects of riveting; the correct answers should be indicated as explained on page 37.

1 The rivet head shown in the sketch is described as:
   a countersunk
   b flat
   c pan
   d cup

JOINING Name: _____ Class: _____ Number: _____

2 The rivet head shown in the sketch is described as:

   a flat
   b pan
   c snap
   d cup

3 The rivet head shown in the sketch is described as:
   a pan
   b cup
   c flat
   d countersunk

4 The rivet head shown in the sketch is described as:
   a cup
   b pan
   c countersunk
   d flat

5 The fault in the riveted joint shown in the sketch was caused by:
   a the rivet being too long
   b the rivet being too short
   c the rivet not being drawn up correctly
   d using a rivet which was too small in diameter

6 The cause of the fault in the riveted joint shown in the sketch is:
   a the rivet being too long
   b the rivet being too short
   c the rivet not being drawn up correctly
   d the rivet being too small in diameter

7 The fault in the riveted joint shown in the sketch was caused by:
   a using a rivet which was too long
   b using a rivet which was too short
   c the rivet not being drawn up properly
   d using a rivet which was too small in diameter

8 The rivet joint shown in the sketch is described as a
   a double strap butt joint
   b single strap butt joint
   c double lap joint
   d single lap joint

9 List FOUR materials suitable for the manufacture of rivets.

10 List FOUR tools required to form, by hand, the heads of the rivets shown in the sketch.

JOINING   Name: _____ Class: _____ Number: _____

11   State TWO advantages of using 'pop' rivets to join pieces of
      material.
_____
_____
_____
_____

12   Explain the difference between a hollow ('pop') rivet and a
      solid shank rivet.
_____
_____
_____

13   State TWO applications of pop riveted joints.
_____
_____
_____

14   Show by means of a sketch what is meant by the terms:
      a   a single-row, riveted lap joint
      b   a single-row, double strap butt joint

15   Describe, with the aid of sketches, how a riveted joint is made by hand, using a snap head rivet. Use a series of sketches to illustrate
      your answer.
_____
_____

16   Explain, with the aid of simple sketches, the sequence of operations used to join two sheets, each of thickness 1 mm, by pop riveting,
      and using hand-operated pliers.
_____
_____

3.d Bolts and screws

The following questions relate to aspects of bolted and screwed joints. The correct answers should be indicated as explained on
page 37.

1   The screw head shown in the sketch is described as:
      a   hexagon
      b   cheese
      c   raised countersunk
      d   countersunk

2   The bolt head shown in the sketch is described as:
      a   pan
      b   cheese
      c   hexagon
      d   instrument

3   The screw head shown in the sketch is described as:
      a   cheese
      b   round
      c   pan
      d   countersunk

      © Stam Press Ltd. Cheltenham, 1987

4 The screw head shown in the sketch is described as:
   a cheese
   b round
   c pan
   d flat

5 The distance advanced by a bolt in one revolution is controlled by the thread:
   a crest
   b depth
   c angle
   d pitch

6 Where the information M30 × 1.5 is given on an engineering drawing it means:
   a a metric thread 30 mm diameter with a pitch of 1.5 mm
   b machine 30 pieces × 1.5 diameter
   c 30 metric threads × 1.5 pitch
   d turn 30 mm diameter with a 1.5 mm chamfer

7 An ISO screw is required, having the following specifications:
   diameter 8 mm, pitch 1.5 mm. This should be shown on an engineering drawing as:
   a 1.5 M × 8
   b M1.5 × 8
   c 8 M × 1.5
   d M 8 × 1.5

8 The angle of a British Standard Whitworth thread is:
   a 30°
   b 47½°
   c 55°
   d 60°

9 A BSP screw thread has a thread angle of:
   a 47½°
   b 55°
   c 60°
   d 65°

10 The thread which has an included angle of 60° is:
   a British Standard Fine
   b ISO Coarse
   c British Association
   d Acme

11 If vibration is continually causing a nut to work loose from a bolt one should use:
   a a plain stud
   b a coarser thread
   c a tab washer
   d a collared stud

12 The locking method which POSITIVELY prevents a nut rotating on a bolt is:
   a lock nut
   b castellated nut with split pin
   c spring washer
   d fibre insert nut

JOINING   Name: —————————————   Class: ————— Number: ———

13 The component shown in the sketch is described as:
   a set screw
   b bolt
   c cap screw
   d stud

Answer questions 14–20 by filling in the missing word or words.

14 A castellated nut is a ——————————— device.

15 The included thread angle of an ISO thread is ———————————.

16 ——————————— nuts contain fibre nylon inserts.

17 The thread locking devices listed in a – d rely on either frictional (F) or mechanical (M) locking.
   Consider each device and indicate alongside whether (F) or (M) applies.
   a standard nut and lock nut ———————————
   b nut and tab washer ———————————
   c single spring washer ———————————
   d nut with nylon insert ———————————

18 The function of a screw thread is to enable rotary motion to be converted to ———————————.

19 Many shakeproof washers must not be filed because some contain beryllium oxide, particles of which are highly———————————.

20 Bolts and screws are identified by diameter, ——————————— of screw thread, length, material and ——————————— of head.

21 Complete the diagram of a thread by writing in the following terms: pitch, major diameter, minor diameter, crest, root (leader lines may be used).

22 State TWO main purposes for which screw threads are widely used in engineering.

23 Explain why a washer should be used under a nut.

24 Name ONE FRICTION and ONE POSITIVE screw joint locking device.

© Stam Press Ltd. Cheltenham, 1987

JOINING   Name: _____   Class: _____   Number: _____

25 Give TWO applications of left-handed threads.

_____
_____

26 Give TWO applications of threaded studs.

_____
_____
_____
_____

27 Identify by name the locking devices illustrated below.

a _____

b _____

c _____

d _____

e _____

28 Name the type of screw in the sketch and give TWO reasons for choosing it in this application.

_____
_____
_____
_____

29 Complete the figure by sketching a hexagon nut and a lock nut in the correct positions:

30 List TWO factors which, when you are selecting a bolt, influence the choice of:

a bolt diameter ———————————————————————————————

———————————————————————————————

———————————————————————————————

b bolt material ———————————————————————————————

———————————————————————————————

———————————————————————————————

c shape of head ———————————————————————————————

———————————————————————————————

———————————————————————————————

31 Make simple sketches to show the differences between slotted head, cross head and socket head screws.
State ONE advantage of each type of head.

a cross head screw ———————————————————

b slotted head screw ———————————————————

c socket head screw ———————————————————

32 Give TWO reasons for the use of a countersunk head screw. ———————————————————————

———————————————————————

———————————————————————

———————————————————————

33 Explain how TWO nuts can be used to give a locking effect. ———————————————————————

———————————————————————

———————————————————————

———————————————————————

3.e Adhesives

The following questions relate to aspects of adhesives. The correct answers should be indicated as explained on page 37. Answer questions 6–9 by filling in the missing word or words.

1 Thermosetting resin adhesives are cured (set) by:
a external heat and pressure
b addition of a catalyst
c cooling from the molten state
d evaporating of a solvent

2 Resin-based adhesives should only be applied in working areas which are:
a small and dust-free
b dark and sealed
c well-ventilated
d well-lit

JOINING   Name: _____   Class: _____   Number: _____

3   One of the most important advantages of joining by thermo-hardening adhesives is that:
    a   it is the cheapest joint possible
    b   the joint is always stronger than a welded joint
    c   high-strength joints may be made between metals and non-metals
    d   the joint can be dismantled easily

4   The adhesive bonded joint shown in the sketch is known as:
    a   butt
    b   inset
    c   strap
    d   lap

5   'Super glues' are:
    a   poor adhesives
    b   poor insulators
    c   quick-acting adhesives
    d   slow-acting adhesives

6   The group of adhesives that undergo a chemical change during curing, and cannot be softened by re-heating, are known as resins.
    _____

7   All adhesives may be classified into two main categories, natural and _____

8   Elastomers are _____ adhesives.

9   'Super glues' are used extensively in the assembly of small_____ components.

10   State TWO hazards associated with the use of adhesives.
    _____
    _____
    _____

11   Describe the method used to make a joint using a contact adhesives.
    _____
    _____
    _____

12   Sketch ONE type of corner joint where adhesives are used.

13   Sketch TWO types of structural stiffeners which may be used to stiffen flat plates and which may be attached to the plates by using adhesives.

    a   b

© Stam Press Ltd. Cheltenham, 1987   46

14 Adhesives are used extensively in modern industry. List FOUR
different applications of adhesives and give reasons for their
selection over other joining methods

————————————————————————
————————————————————————
————————————————————————
————————————————————————
————————————————————————

3.f and g Shrunk and compression joints

The following questions relate to aspects of shrunk and compression joints. The correct answers should be given as explained on page 37.

1 The maximum practical temperature used for hot-shrunk joints is:
a   150°C
b   400°C
c   500°C
d   1000°C

2 The minimum practical temperature used for cold-shrunk joints is:
a   −200°C
b   −150°C
c   −130°C
d   − 90°C

3 State how excessive heating or cooling of mating components
can be avoided.

————————————————————————
————————————————————————
————————————————————————
————————————————————————

4 With reference to compression joints, use simple sketches and brief notes to show the meaning of these terms:

a   external mating surface

————————————————————————
————————————————————————
————————————————————————
————————————————————————
————————————————————————

b   internal mating surface

————————————————————————
————————————————————————
————————————————————————
————————————————————————

5 Explain the purpose of a centring edge on a shaft.

————————————————————————
————————————————————————
————————————————————————
————————————————————————
————————————————————————

6 Explain, with the aid of a simple sketch, how material costs can be reduced by the use of a shrunk joint.

7 Explain, with the aid of a simple sketch, how the use of shrunk joints can save production costs.

8 The sketch shows a part of a cylinder head in section:

    a   State whether hot shrinking or cold shrinking is the most appropriate procedure for inserting the valve seat.

    b   Give the reason for your choice.

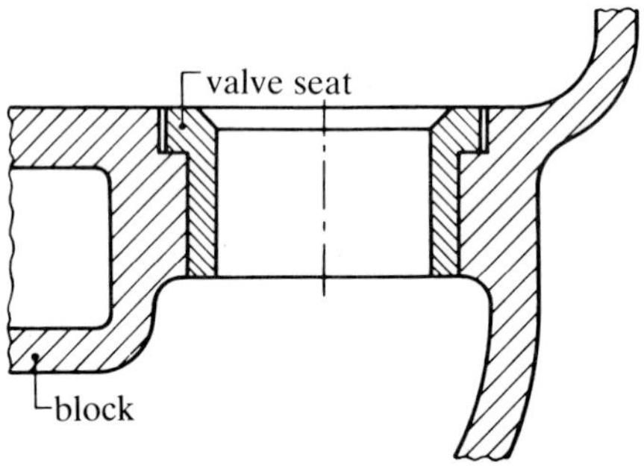

valve seat

block

9 With reference to question 8 explain why it is necessary to use a separate valve seat in the cylinder head.

10 Explain why it is necessary to work quickly when making shrunk joints.

11 State why the amount of interference between components which form a compression joint must be specified.

12 Figures a and b show ball races being fitted:

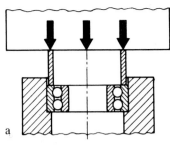 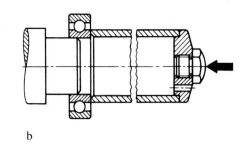

a   b

  a   Why is pressure applied to the outer race only in a?   ——————————————————
——————————————————
——————————————————

  b   What type of equipment would be used to apply the force in b? ——————————————
——————————————————
——————————————————

  c Why, in each case, must pressure be applied at 90° to the   ——————————————————
     finished joint?   ——————————————————
——————————————————
——————————————————

13   The sketch shows a wormwheel. Give THREE reasons why the wheel is unlikely to be made from solid bronze.

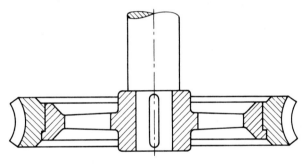

——
——
——
——

14   The sketch in question 13 shows a wormwheeel. Describe how the   ——————————————————
bronze ring is shrunk on to the cast iron body.   ——————————————————
——————————————————
——————————————————
——————————————————

15   List the sequence of operations required to produce a   ——————————————————
compression joint.   ——————————————————
——————————————————
——————————————————
——————————————————

49

3.h Pins and keys

The following questions relate to aspects of pins and keys. In questions 1 to 4 indicate whether a, b, c or d is the correct name of the pin shown in the related figure.

1 a dowel
   b split pin
   c taper pin
   d cotter pin

2 a dowel
   b split pin
   c taper pin
   d cotter pin

3 a straight pin
   b plain pin
   c taper
   d cotter pin

4 a straight pin
   b plain pin
   c taper pin
   d cotter pin

In questions 5, 6 and 7 indicate whether a, b, c or d is the correct name of the key shown in the related figure.

5 a feather
   b gib-head
   c woodruff
   d saddle

6 a feather
   b gib-head
   c woodruff
   d saddle

7 a feather
   b gib-head
   c woodruff
   d saddle

8 Indicate which of the pins a to d is *not* intended to transmit motion:
   a taper
   b dowel
   c split
   d cotter

9 State TWO advantages of a taper pin when compared with
   a parallel pin.

10 Give ONE reason why circlips are made from spring steel.

50

11 State ONE use of a dowel pin.

    ————————————————————
    ————————————————————
    ————————————————————
    ————————————————————

12 State why a safety hazard may be created when a loose fitting
    key is used.

    ————————————————————
    ————————————————————
    ————————————————————
    ————————————————————

13 Show, by means of a sketch and brief notes, a typical application
    of a cotter pin.

51

JOINING   Name: ——————————————— Class: ————— Number: ————

The following questions span the subject matter and approximate to those in the relevant examination paper of the City and Guilds of London Institute. Answers should be short and clear.

1   Sketch and name one example of a:

 a   temporary joint _____

 b   permanent joint _____

 c   flexible joint _____

2   Define a permanent joint.

3   Define soft soldering.

4   State what is needed to ensure a good soft solder bond between two sheets of tinned steel.

5   State TWO advantages that brazing has over soft soldering.

6   State the result of using too hot a flame during the brazing process.

7   State the purpose of the filler rod used in the welding process.

8 State how the flame temperature is controlled in the gas welding process.

9 With the aid of a simple sketch, explain how metal is transferred from the flux-coated electrode to the weld pool.

10 What principle is employed in the spot welding process?

11 List and illustrate with a simple sketch FOUR types of rivet.

12 List the sequence of operations needed to make a riveted joint between two components, using hammer, support dolly and rivet snap.

13 Name the method of riveting best suited for patching thin sheet metal when it is only possible to work from one side.

14 Sketch and clearly illustrate the main features of a bolt.

15 A coarse threaded screw is usually used when it is required to be secured into what type of material?

16 Name TWO circumstances in which a left-hand thread should be used on a bolt or stud.

17 State ONE advantage that a socket head screw has over a slotted or cross-head screw.

18 State TWO reasons for using a threaded stud and nut rather than a bolt to secure components.

19 Name ONE limitation to the use of a self-locking nut.

20 Explain, with the aid of a sketch, the use of a tab washer.

21 List TWO primary uses of natural adhesives.

22 List TWO factors affecting an adhesive bond.

23 Explain, with the aid of a sketch, how a ring may be shrink-fitted on to a shaft.

24 List TWO reasons for using shrunk joints.

JOINING   Name: —————————————————— Class: ——————— Number: ———————

25 Explain what is meant by the term 'interference' as applied to joining by compression.

26 Explain, with the aid of a sketch, the reason for using a centring edge when making a compression joint.

27 Explain, with the aid of a sketch, how a taper pin will positively locate a shaft correctly with a mating part.

28 Explain, with the aid of a sketch, ONE application of a cotter pin.

29 State the purpose of fitting a key between a wheel and a shaft.

30 List THREE different types of key used for joining a component to a circular shaft.

© Stam Press Ltd. Cheltenham, 1987